Today there are more than

three hundred kinds of sharks.

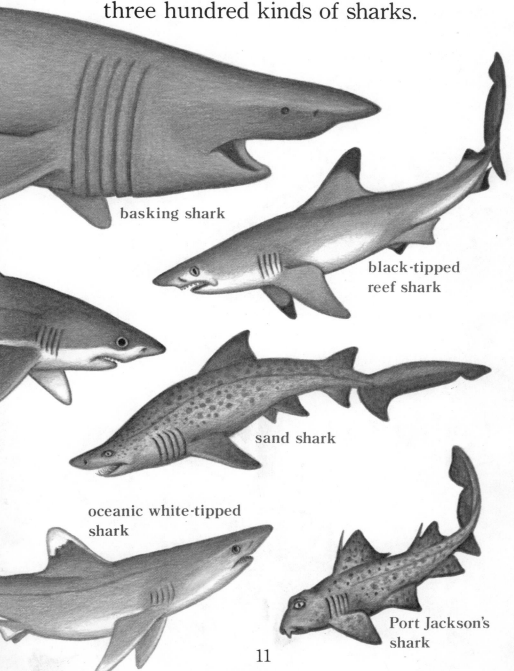

basking shark

black-tipped
reef shark

sand shark

oceanic white-tipped
shark

Port Jackson's
shark

Not all sharks are big.

Many, many kinds

are less than three feet long.

The dwarf shark is no bigger

than your hand.

The small carpet shark lies

on the ocean floor

like a rug.

The leopard shark has spots.

It grows to be about four feet long.

The biggest shark
is the whale shark.
It is longer than a bus.
The whale shark
has three thousand teeth.
But it will never bite you.
It eats only tiny
shrimp and fish.

The whale shark is very gentle.

A diver can even hitch a ride

on its back.

These are blue sharks.

They are far out at sea

hunting for food.

Suddenly

they pick up

the smell of blood.

The sharks speed up.
They shoot through the water
like torpedoes.
In a few minutes
they find a dead whale.

The blue sharks tear off
big chunks of whale meat.
Now the water is
full of biting sharks.

18

If one shark gets hurt,

the others turn on it.

They will eat that shark too.

In a short time

the whale is all gone.

The sharks swim away.

Nothing is left.

Nothing but bones.

Blue sharks are called
the wolves of the sea.
This is because
they stay together in packs.
Blue sharks often swim
after a ship for days.
A long time ago
sailors thought this meant that
someone was going to die.

Why do blue sharks
<u>really</u> follow ships?
The sharks come
because of noises
from the ship.
Then they stay to eat
garbage that is thrown
into the water.

The most dangerous shark

in the sea

is the great white shark.

It is named after

its white belly.

The teeth of the great white shark
are big and sharp.
Very, very sharp.
It can eat a whole seal
in one bite.
The great white shark is
the size of a speedboat.

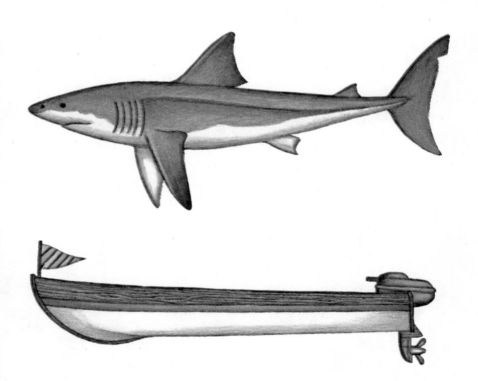

This great white shark

has just had babies.

Most fish lay eggs.

But most sharks do not.

Their babies are born alive.

A baby shark is called a pup.

The pup of the great white shark

is almost the size of a man.

As soon as they are born

the pups go their own way.

It is not safe to stay

near a hungry mother.

The baby sharks swim off
to catch their own food.
One eats a fish.
Another gets a crab.
The pups had better
watch out for puffer fish.

The puffer fish can blow up
like a balloon.
If a shark eats it,
its spines get stuck
in the shark's throat.
The shark will die.

Not many animals

can kill great white sharks.

The stingray

flaps through the sea

like a giant bat.

Its tail has a poison stinger.

The poison can kill most animals.

But a great white shark

can eat a stingray—

stinger and all!

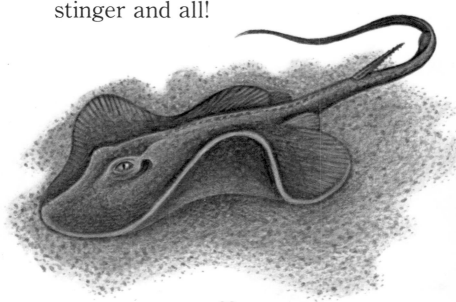

The swordfish is
a very strong fish.
It can cut and stab
with its long nose.
But even a swordfish
almost always loses a fight
with a great white shark.

Another big shark is
the hammerhead shark.
It is easy to see
how it got its name.
Like other big sharks,
the hammerhead never sleeps
and never stops swimming.
Most fish have air balloons
inside them.
But sharks do not.
If they stop swimming,
they sink.

This hammerhead swims
to a group of dolphins.
It tries to catch
one of the young dolphins.
But sharks do not always
get their way.
The dolphins fight back.

One dolphin dives

under the water.

It comes up and

hits the hammerhead.

The shark flies up

in the air.

It falls back on the water.

SMACK!

The dolphins keep
hitting the shark.
After a while
the shark stops moving.
It sinks down into the water.
It is dead.

Dolphins are smart animals.

They can work together

to kill an enemy.

But sharks are not as smart.

They have tiny brains.

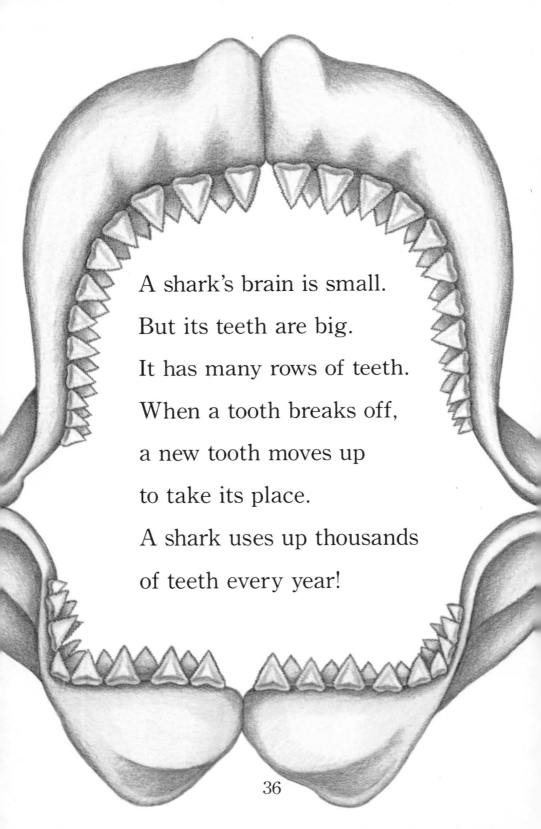

A shark's brain is small.
But its teeth are big.
It has many rows of teeth.
When a tooth breaks off,
a new tooth moves up
to take its place.
A shark uses up thousands
of teeth every year!

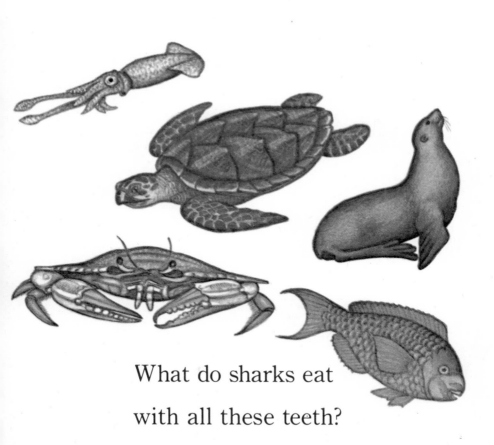

What do sharks eat

with all these teeth?

Fish and more fish.

Other sharks.

Seals,

turtles,

crabs.

Almost anything

that swims in the sea.

Sometimes sharks eat
things that are not food.
No one knows why.
All these things
have been found
inside big sharks:

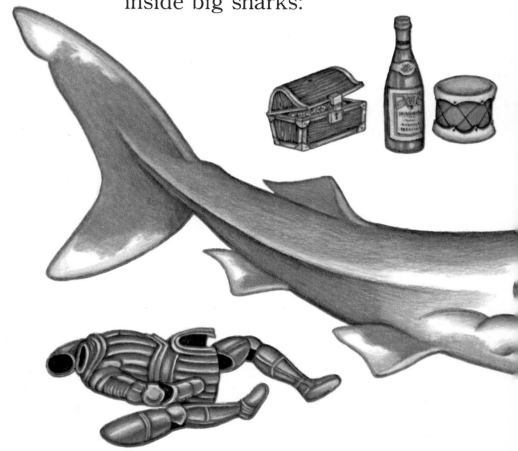

a wallet,

a fur coat,

a drum,

a bottle of wine,

a chest of jewels,

a barrel of nails,

and a suit of armor!

Do sharks eat people?

Yes, they do.

If a person is near a big shark,

the shark may attack.

But the number of people
killed by sharks
is very small.
More people die
from bee stings
than from shark bites!

41

Sharks do not
go hunting for people.
But people do
go hunting for sharks.
Some people like to go
fishing for sharks.
They have to be careful.
A shark may look dead.
Then all at once
it can "wake up"—
and bite!

Scientists want to study sharks.

But it is hard

to study them at sea.

And it is hard to keep

big sharks alive in a tank.

Once scientists caught

a great white shark.

They put it in a tank

with other fish.

But the shark did not eat.

And it kept bumping into

the sides of the tank.

After a few days

the shark began to die.

So the scientists

took the shark back to sea.

They set it free.

There are many things

we do not know about sharks.

We do not know

how long sharks live.

Or how much food

a shark has to eat

to stay alive.

But we do know that sharks

are here to stay.

They are fast and strong.

They hardly ever get sick.

And there is always
plenty of food for them.

As long as there are oceans,
there will be sharks.